God Is in the Heavens of Your Mind

Reality Consciousness

by

Ramadan Muhammad

DORRANCE PUBLISHING CO., INC.
PITTSBURGH, PENNSYLVANIA 15222

All Rights Reserved
Copyright © 1998 by Ramadan Muhammad
No part of this book may be reproduced or transmitted
in any form or by any means, electronic or mechanical,
including photocopying, recording, or by any information
storage and retrieval system without permission in
writing from the publisher.

ISBN # 0-8059-4565-2
Printed in the United States of America

First Printing

For information or to order additional books, please write:
Dorrance Publishing Co., Inc.
643 Smithfield Street
Pittsburgh, Pennsylvania 15222
U.S.A.

TABLE OF CONTENTS

Editor's Two Cents

Introduction

Author's Preface

Part 1...The Groundwork   1
Where Did We Go Wrong?   2
No Progress Without Struggle   4
Mental Slavery   5
Race   5
The Constitution of the Kingdom of God   6
Moral Deviation   7
Martyrdom   9
The "Devil"   10

Part 2... Confused About The Things of This World?   12
Life Through Stages   13
Revelation   15
Nourishment For The Soul   17
Religion In Context   18
What's Real. What's Not   19

Part 3... Practical Matters   26
Qur'an and Bible   27
Leadership   27
Heavenly Knowledge   28
Knowledge is Life   29
Family   30
Model Religion   31
Flesh   33

Part 4...The Path   36
Spiritual Milk   37
Who Are You   39
Knowledge, Then What?   39
The Veil   40
The African American   41
Signs For Those Who Consider   41
Woman   43
The Virtues of Islam   46
The Call   47

Our Supplication

We bear witness that there is none like unto God.

In the name of Allah, Most Gracious, Most Merciful.
Praise be to Allah,
The Cherisher and Sustainer of the Worlds;
Most Gracious, Most Merciful;
Master of the Day of Judgement.
Thee do we worship, and Thine aid we seek.
Show us the straight way,
The way of those on whom Thou hast bestowed Thy Grace,
Those whose (portion) is not wrath,
And who go not astray.

Qur'an 1: 1-7
Surat Al-Fatihah

O Lord, we pray that this modest work is pleasing to you, for that is the only reason we do it. We seek no reward for ourselves other than the satisfaction of knowing that we praised and glorified you and invited others to do the same.

O Lord, forgive us for any errors in this book. We know that your light is bright and pure, but diminishes when refracted through the human soul despite our best efforts to reflect it its full glory.

O Lord, we thank you for your gift of mercy. We are fully aware that it is neither by faith nor by works, but only by Your Grace that anyone may find favor with You.

Editor's Two Cents

When I first read the manuscript for this book, I was overwhelmed by the volume of material that Mister Muhammad had produced over the years. He has covered more ground than most of us cover in a lifetime of contemplation. What you are holding in your hands is what I can only call the sum total of a mere introduction to a vast body of spiritual reflection.

My first challenge was to understand Ramadan's angles. My second challenge was to accept certain principles that were new to me without disturbing my conscience. My third challenge was to present it to you in a simple and digestible format. I must confess that I omitted a lot of information. By the grace of God, we will follow this up with another volume in which we hope to deal with many more specific issues of humanity.

What we hope to do in this book is raise your Reality consciousness above your world consciousness. May God bless Ramadan for writing this material. May God bless you for reading it. It matters not if you have served God all your life, or just met Him yesterday– we all need to be centered and re-centered in God again and again.

The reader should be aware that it is only at the request of the author that I put my name anywhere in this book– *these are the thoughts of Ramadan Muhammad in my words.* Every now and then, as usual, I only offer "my two cents".

Yusef Rashad,
Editor and Contributing Writer

INTRODUCTION

This book reflects on the teachings of Islam (The Qur'an) as well as Christianity (The Bible), and attempts to lessen the gap between them. I believe the reason for this gap is the *mutual* embrace of misinformation, misunderstanding and just plain stubbornness. History is all too often misrepresented, and doctrines are not being challenged by the common person. Religious teachings are founded in fact, but have been obscured in myth and folklore and personality.

Ask the average person about heaven and hell, or the soul, or the afterlife. Where are heaven and hell, if they exist and in what form or manner will we be received? What does the hereafter look like? The only thing that preoccupies our aspirations and our fears more than this world is the afterworld. Yet, we are smothered by false reality in our understanding of either. Our belief or disbelief, correct or incorrect understanding, will determine our fate in this life and the afterlife as well.

The worldly infrastructure has its origin in the minds and egos of men of power and influence. Man has two primary institutions that make this possible; government and religion. Today's predominant civilizations can be traced to Greek-Roman roots of politics, education, art, law, and religion. Of our major languages, Latin and Greek are the main components. This Greek-Roman mind has been the engine behind major powers to this day. No rational person should contend that all politics are evil, but history records a sort of evil consciousness that is prevalent in world governments, because government is the perfect vehicle for less than noble motives.

This book takes a look at the world today. It asks many questions and offers many answers. It offers spiritually based solutions to life's dilemmas. The only way to successfully navigate through life (and the afterlife) is to have a sound relationship with God.

INTRODUCTION

Before a course correction can be offered, we must be made aware that we are headed in the wrong direction. We must also have a clear understanding of how we got off course so we can avoid making the same mistakes again. This, of course, presumes a common destination or goal. So for the sake of argument, this book assumes that we all want peace on earth, peace of mind, knowledge of who we are, and some kind of certainty of our future. With this in mind, I offer the following reasons we are off course:

1. Not being in control: Few recognize just how little control we have over our own thoughts and beliefs, which in turn shape the outcome of our lives. We find ourselves asking, "How did this happen?" Knowing the answer is the first step toward taking control and making course corrections.

2. Having the wrong information: We literally live the information we are given, so we must have correct information to get the desired results. What can be worse than living your life based on a false premise?

3. Tainted doctrine: Everyone's life is governed by doctrine— religious, secular, or otherwise. You must choose your own doctrine after much due consideration and inward reflection, as opposed to passive learning and indoctrination. Study history, read the holy books, ponder life, then decide for yourself.

4. Not knowing who you are: There is history and there is *his*-story. One is fact and the other is interpretation, fancy, or deception. Which one will tell you who you are? We need to hear God's story.

Author's Preface

Before we can even scrutinize our concepts, we should understand what a concept is and how it shapes our lives. Let us arrive at this understanding through illustration. Let us use the concept of "devil" as an example. How would one become devil-like? What qualities does a devil have? Who could tell us what the devil is like so that we could emulate him? Perhaps we could find a devil and ask him? Well, do you see how ridiculous this sounds?

The problem is that we don't realize how ridiculous many concepts are, yet they are at the core of our beliefs and the rules by which we live. The concept of "evil" is treated as an entity with a life of it's own, and the devil is the embodiment of that life. We have given power to this concept simply by acting as if it does have power.

Concepts are ideas or notions inferred by some type of event. We are in a dilemma because we don't understand the extent to which our concepts control our lives, yet at the same time, we want to blame things outside of ourselves for the ills that assault us. *Concepts are subjective evaluations of experience.*

Experience is processed through our subjective mental filters, and our actions take on either negative or positive traits, which we characterize as evil or good. This evil character we have come to think of in terms of spirit. This so-called evil spirit does not really exist, but the concept has power.

Why Did God Create Humans?

God created the human being to worship Him only, and to be spiritually developed by the exercise of will and intelligence. Each of the five senses should be developed in harmony with our spiritual development. We must strike a balance between our material and spiritual development. The brain is the tool by which we maintain the balance between the spiritual and material worlds.

All human beings have a *soul* which comes from God, but the *spirit* is an energy which emits from the soul to be used to accomplish that which is created in the mind, just as the Spirit of God '*moves*', or manifests that which is created in the mind of God. When the individual is in prayer, he is asking God for His grace, and grace emanates from the soul, which is God. Grace is spirit and spirit is a metaphysical form of energy which gives rise to movement in those who receive the Spirit. There is no such thing as a spirit that can harm us. So "devil" is just a concept used to describe a person who is prone to evil expression.

God created human beings for His own pleasure, to watch over them and guide them. He also gave us free will. We have a role to play in this creation. Nothing is born without purpose in this universe. Everything created is in service to God, and He never stops creating.

What is expected of us? What is our service to God? We are to keep the planet in order, and develop ourselves spiritually. Each individual is responsible for his own development. We cannot depend on others for our own spirirual development. How do we develop ourselves spiritually? Well, consider our physical manifestation. We have a body composed of the same elements of its habitat. The body is equipped with five basic senses which are essentially a window between the outer world and the inner world. So logically, these senses seem to have the ability to translate and conduct information between the material and the spiritual. Our spiritual existence is not unlike our material existence. Our soul is composed of the very same elements of its habitat, which is God. Furthermore, the soul is equipped with what might be considered the fleshly sensory counter-parts - eyes, ears, etc. The inner part of our nature is more mysterious than the outer, but not beyond reach, and with the right kind of effort can be developed like our physical bodies.

GOD IS IN THE HEAVENS OF YOUR MIND

The health of body and soul depend on our choices. Health professionals and some medical professionals admonish us for eating foods that slowly kill us, but most of us don't know any better. Well, the prophets (and preachers and teachers from all faiths) share that very same message regarding our souls, and still most of us don't know any better. Just like the body, the soul too lives on what we feed it. We must investigate the source of our sustenance and examine the wisdom of our choices.

The New Covenant

There are two kinds of people in this world; those who keep The Covenant and those who don't. Man was born in debt! To whom is man in debt? To The Creator. How is this debt paid? It is paid with the willful submission to The Creator. The American Heritage Dictionary identifies *'covenant'* as "...God's promise to the human race." That promise is posterity and prosperity and a place in His Book of Life on the condition that man obeys God's law (Genesis, chap. 17 and Revelations, 20:12-15). Yet, the world today, like Moses' people, *"...have turned aside quickly out of the way which I commanded them..."* (Exodus 32:8).

Today's people don't even recognize that they are in debt to our Creator. They don't acknowledge a covenant between God and humanity. For thousands of years, humanity has been flooded with negative influences from every corner of the earth. Ungodliness has become the norm, the preference. The Covenant is like a life insurance policy; upon dying, we are guaranteed a greater benefit than any worldly gain, an incalculable value for the price paid in this life. The new Covenant is really the old Covenant; *submit to the Divine Bendfactor for rightful claim to His Mercy and infinite wealth.*

Part 1
THE GROUNDWORK

GOD IS IN THE HEAVENS OF YOUR MIND

The logical place to start is with a definition of this term "reality" we so often use. The American Heritage Dictionary defines reality as "the quality or state of being actual or true; that which exists objectively and in fact." Your idea of reality is the foundation from which you deal with the world. If God is the source of reality, and if God is to govern your life, then how you live your life should be based on truth. Why do we accept untruths? Why do we allow untruths to control us? This society is not founded on truth. Not much around us is founded on truth. The news, television shows, and cinema are reflections of the untruths that influence us. I believe that true reality consciousness is compromised by this illusory world in which we live. We must return our consciousness to the singular source of reality, which is God. Reality is ever-present and consistent. It confirms what is right and exposes what is false. It can be seen at dusk and seems most prominent when it dawns on us. The only way to check reality is through God.

Where Did We Go Wrong?

God created the heavens and the earth in perfection, and man tore it asunder and brought corruption with his imperfection. The story of Adam is an everyday reality for mankind. Adam was created in a state of purity, without sinful inclinations. He adored his creator and knew not the ways of ungodliness until temptation visited him. There were other players on the stage during Adam's lifetime. Scripture tells us that God Almighty has a vast domain inhabited by countless beings. There is enmity between man and some of these other beings, much the same way there is enmity between men. The infamous Satan, or Iblis as he is known to Muslims, was the first to turn against man.

THE GROUNDWORK

Ironically, Iblis was a very important servant in the kingdom of God. So profound was his service and worship, and so close to the throne of God was he, that the angels took notice of him with respect and admiration. He was a model of worship. God the All-knowing, however, saw into the heart of Iblis and perceived arrogance. When Adam was created, God endowed him with qualities possessed by no other. And though he was in many ways inferior to Iblis and the angels, Adam was made to excel in other ways, such as independence and free will and a certain degree of knowledge not privileged to Iblis and the angels.

The angels were in awe of God's great work, but Iblis was prone to jealousy and conceit. God ordered Iblis and the angels to bow down to Adam out of respect for His great work. The angels obeyed, but Iblis refused saying he would not be made to bow to someone inferior to himself. Secretly, Iblis misled Adam into disobedience, causing them both to fall from grace. Adam asked to be forgiven, while Iblis asked for reprieve, time he would use to try to corrupt all of Adam's offspring and alienate them from grace. They were both granted their request.

So, just as Iblis was once a model of worship in the kingdom of God, he is now *the* model of corruption in this world, turning men's hearts and minds away from God inwardly toward their own passions. And since deviance begets deviance, we do as we see. We now live in a world where deviance is the norm, and the path to God is the exception. It's a mental slave plantation where we cultivate crops for the flesh while we starve the soul. The harvest of this world is toxic.

However, just as Adam sought forgiveness and returned to God, so can the offspring of Adam. By way of Adam, God demonstrates His Mercy and Kindness to those who prefer the company of God.

GOD IS IN THE HEAVENS OF YOUR MIND

Man started out in truth on the path of godliness, but the glitter of materialism and the allure of worldly life and the convincing argument of Satan has warped his judgement and amplified his carnal appetites. It takes keen spiritual eyes to see that we are caught in a tug of war between the "Godly mind" and the "Satanic mind". Everything and everyone is influenced by one or the other. There is no neutral ground. God intends for man to live righteously and receive His mercy. Satan wants to cut man off from God and snare him into the trap of false security. Satan is always looking for opportunities to take advantage of the unaware, the confused, the stubborn-minded, the misguided, and the worldly individual. Knowing is half the battle, and knowing that someone has a vested interest in your failure is enough to put you on guard, sharpen your judgement, and help you make better choices.

No Progress Without Struggle

Nature teaches us that nothing in this world exists outside the realm of struggle, but after struggle comes ease. For example, birth is a struggle for mother and child. They both struggle to bring new life into the world. The child struggles to inflate his lungs for the first time. So it is with everything in life, especially spiritual life. Coming out of the darkness into the spiritual awakening is a struggle. Wrestling your mind away from worldliness is a struggle. But after struggle comes ease. Sharper judgement and better choices in how you live your life make any struggle more bearable and the path to ease shorter. Spiritual struggle is not without reward. Again and again in various religious scriptures and traditions we are taught that God places no burden on any soul that it cannot bear, and the rewards of spiritual struggle are beyond man's measure!

THE GROUNDWORK

Mental Slavery

The American Heritage Dictionary, defines slavery as, " 3. the condition of being subject or addicted to a specified influence." Hundreds of years after the fact, African Americans are still hung up on slavery, and generations later, still wrestling with its adverse effects on the social psyche. This is also true of white America. So much baggage has been carried over from the past, such as fear and hatred. We feared and hated the slavemaster, and now we hate his descendants and vice versa. Old hostilities and barriers are perpetuated.

Emotion is not rational, so fear and hatred are not products of rational thought. That same hate and fear can easily be translated into love and trust. This is self-evident. In spite of a fragmented society, to an ever-increasing degree we are indelibly integrated in mind, body, and spirit. In many ways, whites and non-whites are moving toward each other, not away.

We must release that old baggage lest we become enslaved by the manipulating hand of our mutual enemy, the Satanic mind, that seeks to divide us, turning us one against the other, thereby losing our humanity and forfeiting our redemption.

Race

Prophet Muhammad (peace and blessings to him), whom Muslims hold to be the last of God's prophets among mankind, said that in the last days we would be led by the descendants of slaves. This is obvious all over the world where Jews and Arabs and Africans and African Americans and myriad of "nations of color"— once enslaved nations— now sit in high places and shape world events.

Now we must find our way back to God, who promised He would bring a new kingdom and preside over it Himself. God does not need a palace or actual real estate from which to rule, although He does promise to revamp the current real estate. However, *you* are the temple, the landscape from which God will rule! Traditionally, we envision the kingdom of God as some celestial place, but we should instead turn our sight to the inner space. If God's kingdom was established in the heart and soul of every person, it would be manifest outwardly and this would be a holy and godly world throughout. That's what God means when He says He will establish His kingdom; He will populate the land with hearts and souls in which He abides and rules.

The Constitution of the Kingdom of God

Consider your personal rules. Everyone has them. You have certain ideas about how people should or should not treat you, and how people should or should not behave toward one another. If you share housing or land with someone, you each have specific rules of etiquette. You must agree on many complex issues regarding the handling of your personal space as well as the environment you share. Ideally, people of like minds and inclination flock together and live in harmony. But the world is a labyrinth of different shades of personalities and inclinations ad infinitum, making it impossible for all to agree on a single code of ethics, etiquette, or morality.

Who is better capable or more qualified to conceive a universal code of ethics than He who created man, the One ever present and consistent reality? None! So, naturally it follows, that only God can say what is morally deviant. After all, God is the inventor of morality. His word is the measure of all things. He is the source of goodness and the origin of righteousness; so anything that deviates from Him, deviates from what is good and right.

Let's ask ourselves, what type of person or people would God trust with this code of ethics? Who would you put in charge of something valuable and significant? The answer should be someone who is of uncompromising character; an honest, loyal, sincere, humble person who believes in your cause and is inclined to serve. Who knows the heart better than God? He gives special individuals a special trust. Special individuals are chosen to reveal God's message. His message is the Constitution, a penal code, a comfort and guide for mankind, a record of man's past, a confirmation of man's purpose and destiny, and insight into God himself. The messengers we call prophets. The message we call revelation. When revelation is put into writing, we call it scripture. The primary and most well-known scriptures were revealed through the descendants of one of the most revered prophets of all time, Abraham. Much of early revelation found its way into what Christians today call the Bible. Muslims believe that the last revelation, the Qur'an, came through the last prophet, Muhammad. The Qur'an is considered to be the only scriptures to survive untainted and complete.

Moral Deviation

In the Holy Book of God, Al Qur'an, it is said that if there are two persons among you who practice lewdness, bear witness against them about their lewdness and punish them. If they repent and amend, leave them alone. If they continue, then you must run them away from you (Qur'an 4:15-18). The bible (KJV) says,

> *"Be not deceived: evil communications corrupt good manners. Awake to righteousness, and sin not; for some have not the knowledge of God: I speak this to your shame"*
> *(1 Corinthians 15:33-34),*

> *"...if any man is called a brother be a fornicator, or covetous, or an idolater, or a railer, or a drunkard, or an extortioner, with such a one do not eat"*
> *(1 Cor 5:11),*

> "Beware lest any man spoil you through philosophy and vain deceit, after the tradition of men, after the rudiments of the world, and not after Christ"
> (Colossians 2:8),

> "Enter not into the path of the wicked, and go not in the way of evil men. Avoid it, pass not by it, turn from it, and pass away. For they sleep not, except they have done mischief; and their sleep is taken away, unless they cause some to fall. For they eat the bread of wickedness and drink the wine of violence. But the path of the just is as the shining light, that shineth more and more unto the perfect day"
> (Proverbs 4:14-17),

> "And have no fellowship with the unfruitful works of darkness, but rather reprove them"
> (Ephesians 5:11),

The Qur'an aptly complements these verses with the following:

> "By (time), Verily man is in loss, except such as have faith, and do righteous deeds, and (join together) in the mutual teaching of Truth, and of Patience and Constancy."
> (Q 103:1-3)

Again and again, God reminds us to stay away from those who deviate, and to keep company with those who seek righteousness. Why? Because those who deviate will beckon you to corruption, while those who seek righteousness will beckon you to God. We must be especially careful to guard our children from the influence of the covetous, the fornicator, the idolater, the drunkard, the homosexual, the liar, the cheater, the thief, and so on. The drug user and dealer want to get you high. The fornicator will solicit unlicensed sex with you. The cheater wants you to help him defraud people and betray your spouse. The homosexual wants to twist nature to suit his taste and violate your body. Divine scripture very clearly and in no uncertain terms states that these acts are displeasing to God. Some acts He refers to as an abomination:

> *"These six things doth the Lord hate: yea, seven are an abomination unto Him: A proud look, a lying tongue, and hands that shed innocent blood, An heart that deviseth wicked imaginations, feet that be swift in running to mischief, A false witness that speaketh lies, and he that soweth discord among brethren."*
> *(Proverbs 6:16-19)*

> *"Ye are they which justify yourselves before men: but God knoweth your hearts: for that which is highly esteemed among men is abomination in the sight of God."*
> *(Luke 16:15)*

So God's advice and warning is to avoid the tempter so that the hand of temptation cannot reach you.

Martyrdom

Let us again reach into the American Heritage Dictionary where we find "martyr 2. One who makes great sacrifices or suffers much in order to further a belief, cause, or principle." Typically, we think of a martyr as someone who actually dies for a cause, but in the context of this definition, we can say that a martyr is anyone who sacrifices his own needs and desires for a greater cause. One who sincerely gives up self for God is worthy of martyrdom. Giving up drugs and alcohol, promiscuity, vanity, and materialism, or whatever one may be attached to, for the service of God is true martyrdom. Sometimes the tempter is your neighbor, your friend, your relative, or even yourself. Sometimes the temptation can seem like the most natural thing in the world. However, the prophets showed us by example that anything other than service and submission to God is frivolous and unnatural.

Submission requires selflessness and tremendous resolve. It also requires love, but how can you love that which you do not know. So one must become acquainted with God and cultivate a relationship based on trust and faith, humbling oneself and subduing all self-centered motives and devoting one's life to God. What greater sacrifice can one make but to give up the self? What cause is greater than God's cause?

The "Devil"

The typical concept of the Devil as taught in many traditions is that of a sinister looking fellow who dwells deep in the bowels of the earth where he is the administrator of unspeakable horrors. Often depicted as some kind of man-animal hybrid, he is man's worst nightmare! However, the Devil is more a state of mind than some hideous monster who presides over a fiery subterranean graveyard. Iblis himself (Satan) is nothing more than a once-righteous being who later adopted a devilish state of mind. Seeing how easily we seduce each other into evil, it's not hard to imagine the power of the unseen seducer:

> *"O ye Children of Adam! Let not Satan seduce you, in the same manner as he got your parents out of the Garden, stripping them of their raiment, to expose their shame: for he and his tribe watch you from a position where ye cannot see them: We made the Evil Ones friends (only) to those without Faith."*
> *(Q 7:27)*

THE GROUNDWORK

Difficult as it is to relate to in this day and age, there was a time when anyone who questioned religious doctrine was dealt with harshly, especially if that person openly challenged prevailing thought. Many people were slain in the name of God. So-called heresy was not taken lightly. Religious dogma was the law of the land. So when the church said God was up above and Satan was down below, few questioned it. This dogma became indelibly etched into the psyche of mankind. It's in our songs, our literature, our children's storybooks, and so forth.

These days, however, dogma is challenged and questioned. Unfortunately, truth is often rejected along with falsehood.

Part 2

CONFUSED ABOUT THE THINGS OF THIS WORLD?

CONFUSED?

The key to human development is the cultivation of the spirit. As we develop spiritually, life's perplexities unravel. Knowledge is power, and that is why it is so elusive! God did not make it easy to unlock the mysteries of life. One of the ways that evil-minded people are constrained within limits is by keeping them in ignorance. Higher knowledge is gained through spiritual development. God chooses to entrust such higher understanding to those who fear Him and respect His creation.

The first step in such growth is to always be aware of God's presence through prayer and praise. Also, do not mistreat others, adhere to moral conduct and take responsibility for your actions. These simplistic things go a long way in life. We must make the right choices. Even the simplest choices matter, like our choice of food, clothing, education, entertainment, the company we keep, and the products we buy. It is said, that one page of text is equal to about six hours of television. Yet, we value entertainment over knowledge. We hurt ourselves by not learning all we can in this life. God does not want us to live and die without knowing the truth about our journey here.

Life Through Stages

Contrary to popular psychology, the mind is whole, not fragmented into the conscious and the unconscious. What Jung[1] referred to as the collective unconscious is, I believe, God.

Just as our bodies coexist in a common environment, genetically linked to each other, sustained by the same elements, in a universe nestled in the thoughts of God, so it is on the mental and spiritual planes. We reside within God and He resides within us,

---

1. Carl Gustav Jung was one of the eminent founders of modern psychology and psychoanalysis who originated many profound theories. He coined the phrase "collective unconscious", which he describes as consisting of mythological themes or primordial images he called "archetypes". He believed that this collective unconscious is a singular mind shared by all humans unperceived by the conscious mind. (read The Essential Jung, Princeton Books).

GOD IS IN THE HEAVENS OF YOUR MIND

He is alone in His unique existence, but He manifests through creation, inwardly as well as outwardly.

The physical body experiences God's manifestation in the conscious universe, but the soul experiences God's manifestation in the unconscious universe, the incorporeal realm where all souls abide together in God as the bodies abide together in God in this realm. This is why Jung observed that all themes which proceed forth from the unconscious are universal. For example, seeing a tree is a universal experience; we've all seen one. Social interaction is a universal experience; we all do it. These simple examples are possible because we share a common environment. And so it is in the unconscious world, which is another facet of the overall singular manifestation of God. If we could experience both worlds through pure perception (and we don't), we would transcend our limited thinking. This is possible by the cultivation of the spirit, increasing your God-awareness through prayer and constant remembrance of God in every moment, contemplating His word in scripture, living and working by faith and surrendering to no influence except His. This is reality consciousness, being centered in God, not the world.

Reality consciousness comes in stages, however. One must first become acquainted with God through scripture and prayer and by pondering His work, His creation. Then comes acceptance. Then comes a transformation of one's way of life. Then one begins to serve God, doing work for God. And as your relationship with God grows, love, trust, and faith grows. And only after love, trust and faith have established themselves in your heart, does true worship begin. Reality consciousness evolves with each stage, bringing the servant ever closer to the Master.

Revelation

All revelation comes from God to a select few, who are entrusted to teach it to others. God reveals only what He wants us to know. Scripture tells us that Jews, Christians, Buddhists, Muslims, etc., all originate from the same revelations. But men tamper with revelation (or our understanding of revelation) and lead many astray. This is why it is very important that we understand the significance of prophethood. Many come, but few are chosen! Only the righteous among us are chosen by God to be His prophets.

The heart must be open to God and ready to serve God willingly and lovingly. The soul must be ready to put its own life on the line for God. Revelation must be sent through a pure and trustworthy vehicle. Prophets are souls who attain great spiritual heights and devotion. They are privy to knowledge that the rest of us are not. They have a deep understanding that distinguishes them from false prophets. False prophets cannot move the world as true prophets do because God has not given them such power and authority. Following someone who is not teaching the true revelation of God, will only lead you to ignorance and error. This is why we must put our trust in those who brought revelation and taught us its meaning.

> "He granteth wisdom to whom He pleaseth; And he to whom wisdom is granted receiveth indeed a benefit overflowing; But none will grasp the Message except men of understanding."
> (Q 2:269)

> "...no one knows its true meanings except Allah (God)...
> (Q 3:7)

> "When it is said to them; Come to what Allah (God) hath revealed; come to the Messenger: They say; 'Enough for us are the ways we found our fathers following.' What! even though their fathers were void of knowledge and guidance?" (Q 5:104)

> "And commemorate Our Servants Abraham, Isaac and Jacob, possessors of power and vision. Verily We did choose them for a special (purpose) - proclaiming the Message of the Hereafter. They were, in Our sight, truly of the company of the Elect and the Good." (Q 38:45-47)

> "Therefore let whoso will, keep it in remembrance, it is in books held greatly in honour, exalted in dignity, kept pure and holy, written by the hands of scribes- honourable and pious and just. (Q 80:12-16).

No prophet chose his calling, nor shall we choose our own calling. God grooms each of us for whatever He ordains for us. Since all things return to Allah (God), then we are all on the path to God.

Consider the path of the prophets. They start out spiritually undeveloped as we all do. Either they perceive the beckoning of the Lord or they already have it in their hearts to seek Him out. With God's guidance, they transcend themselves and this world through the purification of their hearts and the cultivation of their God-awareness. Only through challenge, sacrifice, and dedication can a soul attain spiritual heights. The prophets of old taught us how to apply this principle in our lives.

Nourishment For The Soul

The mind and soul are a type of digestive system. As the saying goes, you are what you eat. In other words, your body is only as good as what you put in it. Within that context, the body has an amazing wisdom and capacity for extracting what it needs from what you feed it. It filters out as much bad stuff as it can, and absorbs the good stuff. God built this wisdom into your body and it requires no conscious effort on your part, except that you use good judgement in your choice of diet, eating the food that promotes good health.

Your mind and soul work along the same principle, except in this case, it very much requires a conscious effort on your part. You are what you eat. Your mind and soul are only as good as the stuff you put into them. What you take in becomes your identity, your reality. Again, this is Reality Consciousness. Your mental and spiritual diet become the building blocks of your inner environment. We should love to keep that environment clean and pure, for *"God loves those who make themselves pure"* (Q 9:108).

So, the obvious question arises; what is pure nourishment for the mind and soul? Consider the statement made earlier, that scripture tells us we are basically all the same and there is only one revealed religion, but man tampers with revelation. From this we can draw an analogy. There is only one source of food, the earth. Man takes from the ground that which is pure and wholesome, and for whatever reason, he processes it, causing a degradation of much of its nutritional value. In the process, artificial elements are added while much of the valuable elements are removed. And so it is with scripture and revelation. Man takes from the mouths of prophets that which is pure, and for what ever reason, corrupts it through his mental and social processes, introducing elements not of the original while removing valuable elements of truth. In many instances, revelation is turned into a "cult of personality", whereby ego and personal slants color the message.

Thus, we have the challenge of carefully screening what we put into our system of beliefs. We must filter out the wrong stuff and absorb the right stuff. *"And verily in cattle will ye find an instructive Sign. From what is within their bodies, between excretions and blood, We produce, for your drink, milk, pure and agreeable to those who drink it."... (Q 16:66)*. We must seek the milk of spiritual sustenance. We must not lean upon our own understanding, but rather seek guidance from Him who grants wisdom and provides sustenance. We must follow the example of those in the company of the good and elect, the pious and the just, whom God chose from amongst ourselves as *spiritual role models*.

Religion in Context

Our word "religion" has latin origins- religio, meaning "respect for what is sacred, awe", rooted in the verb "religare", to bind. As Charles Panati points out in his book 'Sacred Origin of Profound Things', "In Medieval Europe, the word [religion] evolved to mean 'a system of sacred beliefs and practices that binds a people together' ". (p vii) This underlying principle of religio/religare encompasses every aspect of man's existence. This is a very powerful notion, skillfully exploited by the Satanic mind and world governments. If you can control a people's belief system, power, wealth, and fame will be your intimate companions.

Basically, man defends four things; his life, his loved ones, his property, and his god (or ideology). These are the things that are sacred to man, the things that "...bind a people together". What is government but a sovereignty of sacred things? It is the culmination of the belief system of an extended family and the protection of their rights and properties... *"I pledge allegiance to the flag of the United States of*

America, and to the Republic for which it stands; one nation under God, indivisible, with liberty and justice for all" (The Pledge of Allegiance).

This is fundamental to every human being anywhere in the world. Everyone belongs to a belief system. Your belief system is like the immune system. It protects you from anything that it considers to be a threat to your reality. We're all indoctrinated one way or the other, and anything that is not consistent with your belief system is like a disease. The Satanic mind cannot get to you without first compromising the very thing that protects you— your belief system. If your immune system can be made to degenerate, you're left vulnerable to ill influences. Sound like spiritual AIDS? That's exactly what it is, but we can overcome it through prayer, guidance, and Reality Consciousness.

What's Real, What's Not?

Unfortunately, it's difficult to see the universality and value of religion when there is so much discord and dysfunction in religion. However, it's not the message that's defective, it's the bottle. Every religion claims that the other is compromised. Let's examine that for a moment.

> *"And the Lord said unto him, Who hath made man's mouth? or who maketh the dumb, or deaf, or the seeing, or the blind? have not I the Lord? Now therefore go, and I will be with thy mouth, and teach thee what thou shalt say.*
> *(Exodus 4:11-12)*

> *"He that loveth me not, keepeth not my sayings: and the word which ye hear is not mine, but the Father's which sent me."*
> *(John 14:24)*

> "Muhammad is no more than a Messenger: many were the Messengers that passed away before him..."
> (Q 3:144)

> "Allah [God] did confer a great favour on the Believers when He sent among them a Messenger from among themselves, rehearsing unto them the signs of Allah, sanctifying them, and instructing them in Scripture and Wisdom, while before that, they had been in manifest error."
> (Q 3:164)

As already stated, man takes from the mouths of prophets that which is pure and changes it. Why? Because the Satanic influence wants to compromise your belief system.

> "Ye shall not add unto the word which I command you, neither shall ye diminish ought from it, that ye may keep the commandments of the Lord your God which I command you."
> (Deuteronomy 4:2)

> "...and this people shall rise, and go a whoring after the gods of the strangers of the land, whither they go to be among them, and will forsake me, and break my covenant which I have made with them. Then my anger shall be kindled against them in that day, and I will forsake them, and I will hide my face from them, and they shall be devoured, and many evils and troubles shall befall them..."
> (Deut. 31:16-17)

> "And such as Allah [God] doth guide there can be none to lead astray."
> (Q 39:37)

Consider Israel. Not long after the death of Moses, she took into herself strange gods to worship. She raised up kings to rule her. Soon, corrupt men got a stronghold on her and the laws and teachings of Moses were obscured, diluted, and often rejected altogether. God told Moses that this would happen, and what consequences it would bring. Then peoples of another tongue conquered Israel, raped and mutilated her culture and belief system.

Consider Jesus. The powers that be (Rome), tried to assassinate him and tried to assassinate his teachings. But when his following became too widespread and popular to contain, Rome and her bedfellows brought Christendom into their bedroom, and out of egocentrism, paternalistic chauvinism, political arrogance, and just plain ignorance, they furtively raped, pillaged, and vandalized the teachings of Jesus. Like so much revelation, the original gospel was lost between politics and war. Christendom became hot government property.

During this time, trade was a major factor in the social and political scheme of things. Religious and cultural lines were blurred. Due to political pressures, concessions in matters of religious doctrine were made constantly. Sometimes right ideas were omitted, and other times foreign ideas were assimilated. The prime example of this is the concept of the Trinity, introduced into Christianity only in fairly recent history. Islam as well suffered the influence of European trade and politics. And the further removed from the prophet, the more diluted the message.

It's like the game where one person whispers something into the ear of another person, and that message is passed around the room in like manner. By the time it returns to the person with whom it started, the message is almost unrecognizable. Then that person sets the record straight. The prophets will at some time, set the record straight:

> *"One day We shall raise from all peoples a witness: then will no excuse be accepted from unbelievers nor will they receive any favours."*
> *(Q 16:84)*

> *"Then shall We question those to whom Our Message was sent and those by whom We sent it. And verily We shall recount their whole story with knowledge, for We were never absent."*
> *(Q 7:6-7)*

> *"Which when the apostles, Barnabas and Paul, heard of, they rent their clothes, and ran in among the people, crying out, And saying, 'Sirs, why do ye these things? We also are men of like passions with you, and preach unto you that ye should turn from these vanities unto the living God, which made heaven, and earth, and the sea, and all things that are therein: Who in times past suffered all nations to walk in their own ways. Nevertheless, He left not Himself without witness, in that He did good, and gave us rain from heaven, and fruitful seasons, filling our hearts with food and gladness."*
> *(Acts 14:14-17)*

When God is ready to call mankind to account, prophets will be brought forth to bear witness against the crowd as to the message that was preached. They will set the record straight.

> *"And this gospel of the kingdom shall be preached in all the world for a witness unto all nations; and then shall the end come."*
> *(Matthew 24:14)*

> *"Nay, this is a Glorious Qur'an (Inscribed) in a Tablet Preserved"*
> *(Q 85:21-22)*

> *"By degrees shall We teach thee to declare (the Message), so thou shalt not forget..."*
> *(Q 87:6).*

Although the fundamental precepts remain intact, revelations brought by prophets were not preserved in their original state, neither in written form nor in oral traditions. No serious religious scholar disputes it. Even authorship is in question. The Qur'an is the only exception. Even non-Muslim scholars don't dispute that Muhammad is the sole person responsible for introducing the Qur'an to humanity. Furthermore, ancient preserved copies of the Qur'an, as well as documented history, confirm the assertion that the Qur'anic scriptures that we recite today are the original scriptures recited by Muhammad 1400 years ago. It is as good as hearing the words come directly from his own mouth. So, not only will God bring forth prophets to bear witness, but also the gospels which they left behind, foremost of which is the Qur'an, well-preserved. And these holy books will bear witness against mankind.

You might be wondering, why, if they have the word of God, don't Muslims have a utopian society? Because Muslims don't live in a vacuum. There are tremendous tugs of cultural currents, and winds of social change that sweep through the heart. However, what may be lacking in the outer world can be sought after in the inner world:

> *"And We will make it easy for thee (to follow) the simple (path). Therefore give admonition in case the admonition profits (the hearer). The admonition will be received by those*

who fear (Allah): But it will be avoided by those most unfortunate ones...but those will prosper who purify themselves, and glorify the name of their Guardian Lord, and (lift their hearts) in Prayer."
(Q 87:8-15).

"By the Soul, and the proportion and order given to it; and its enlightenment as to its wrong and its right- Truly he succeeds that purifies it, and he fails that corrupts it!"
(Q 91:7-10)

"Those who faithfully observe their trusts and covenants; and who (strictly) guard their prayers- these will be the heirs, who will inherit Paradise."
(Q23:8-11)

"We are your protectors in this life and in the Hereafter: Therein shall ye have all that your souls shall desire; therein shall ye have all that ye ask for!- A hospitable gift from One Oft-Forgiving, Most Merciful!"
(Q 41:31-32).

If we guard our covenant with God, we will find utopia within our individual selves. There are those who turn away from God and create their world according to their preferences. And though we live in the midst of confusion and uncertainty, peace is found in God and His promise.

Heaven is to be found on earth, in us, if we live according to God's design. Heaven resides in our universe among the galaxies of His vast creation.

Part 3
PRACTICAL MATTERS

Qur'an and Bible

One of the greatest misconceptions within and without the religious community, is that the Qur'an and the Bible teach a different religion. The truth is both are revelations from God. Both teach the same fundamental principles, foremost of which are the Oneness of God (or His supreme and unique sovereignty), His angels, His prophets, the hereafter, the laws of God, His mercy, and the need for prayer. There is only one religion; submission to the One God! What we see today is the fragmentation of this message, where someone whispers, "Submit to the One God", and by the time it gets across the room, or across generations, it ends up as "Submit to the Father, the Son, and the Holy Ghost".

So many influences come into play in between. Every cook flavors the stew in his own fashion, according to his vain tastes or misdirected fervor. Doctrine is supposed to leave an imprint on the people, but every generation leaves its imprint on doctrine. Even educated, enlightened, God-fearing people with good intentions make this mistake.

Leadership

Consider the Israelites. When Moses took them out of Egypt, they wandered a great many years in the desert before finally possessing a land of their own. During this interim, God, through Moses, taught them self-sufficiency and leadership. They were large in number and required cohesiveness and organization. So God appointed Moses as overall judge and leader. The nation was then divided into twelve tribes according to genealogy, each one having an appointed leader. Within each tribe there were trustees appointed over various smaller groups or tasks. The law, as it was revealed to Moses, was taught to every leader, who in turn taught it to the people in his charge. Furthermore, every leader hand-picked his own successor and groomed him for the role. So a very large community was made manageable and productive by empowering smaller groups with knowledge, a guiding principle, God-consciousness, and leadership training. These are the tools of preparation and greatness. The whole became greater than the sum total of its parts.

Our society today is sorely divided, from the family on up. God-consciousness is not a required course in the average home and leadership training for our youth is left to a particular roll of the dice, or fate, more or less. Furthermore, we have lost touch with the wisdom of God, who established specific roles to ensure harmony and balance. Our sexual identity and our familial structure and social values have all become quite warped and defaced. We are out of sync with each other and out of sync with Reality (God). Reality Consciousness is obscured beneath layers and eons of materialism, attachment, ignorance, lust, and vanity. So it's no wonder that our leadership reflects the tone of the times rather than the image of God, with clergy and religious groups in general often proving to be some of the worst case scenarios!

Heavenly Knowledge

Man is capable of reaching great heights of wisdom and spirituality. Where can wisdom come from but God? His wisdom and mercy are the nectar of Heaven, the food of all creation. God is the source of all knowledge. Most of us are content with worldly knowledge. Worldly knowledge is only a steppingstone to heavenly knowledge. Scientific method teaches us to start with the event or manifestation or evidence, and trace it back to its origin. Using this logic, we can start with the manifestation (all of creation that we are able to observe), and trace it back to its origin (the Cause that we call God). It's interesting to note, that some people contend that this all came about spontaneously in the absence of Divine Presence or intelligent manipulation, and out of this divine-less and unintelligent event can arise intelligent beings with an innate impulse to discover its divine origin.

This impulse is the beginning of our heavenly quest. And though we can never grasp the creator, we can get a glimpse of Him through His creation. This is the beginning of heavenly knowledge. Heaven is a state of being beyond mind, brain and body, but unattainable without the purification of mind and body. Through righteousness, mental and physical purity, intelligent use of our faculties, and Reality Consciousness, we come into a heavenly state of being. None but those of pure spirit, humble and obedient heart and mental fitness may enter into heaven; not those who follow their lusts and wallow in decadence and vanities.

Knowledge is Life

Complacency and stagnancy sap the life right out of us. There are infinite opportunities to gain knowledge that require very little effort, yet many people are too complacent. We are literally surrounded by knowledge. It's like a person who works in a bookstore or library and never opens a book. What he reads could change his life forever, or at least provide him with the missing link of the solution to a challenge he may be facing. But knowledge is only potential and has no value if it is not applied.

Having knowledge and not putting it to work is like not having it at all. There is no growth, no motion, no benefit. God never places anyone in any situation without surrounding him with useful knowledge and resources within his reach.

Interesting to note, is the disproportionate relation of African Americans to other groups in higher education. The scales are badly, sadly unbalanced. This is a symptom of blurred inner vision and low self-worth that plagues the African American community. The areas in which this race of people primarily excel (such as sports and entertainment), do not elevate them on the whole as can higher learning, both worldly and spiritual.

The Family

Let's put the wisdom of God under scrutiny. As mentioned before, God established specific roles for everything in relation to everything else. He set creation in a certain balance and proportion. He gave us guidelines by which to live. For his sake? Certainly not, for how does marriage and monogamy and chastity and charity and so forth benefit Him? And how does our pursuit of heavenly knowledge benefit the source of all knowledge? It does not benefit Him in any way. It's for *our* sake!

Consider the family unit. God created man, set him on a path of spiritual bliss, fashioned a mate for him, and put love between them. Only the union of a man and woman can produce a child. And only out of a loving union can a well-balanced, well-rounded individual grow.

> *"Oh mankind! reverence your Guardian Lord, Who created you from a single person, created, of like nature, his mate, and from them twain scattered (like seeds) countless men and women...and reverence the wombs that bore you..."*
> *(Q 4:1)*

> *"It is He Who created you from a single person, and made his mate of like nature, in order that he might dwell with her*

(in love). When they are united, she bears a light burden and carries it about..."
(Q 7:189)

Trying to raise happy and well-adjusted children, especially in this day and age, is challenging to say the least. Raising them in a one-parent situation is like trying to win a hundred-meter dash with one leg. Single parents just cannot compete with whole, healthy families. It's challenging even for two-parent families. You must take an active role in the overall development of your children, being careful not to neglect any facet of their lives, be it physical, emotional, social, intellectual, or spiritual. Parents are the blueprints from which their children are fashioned. Family and personal identity goes beyond the family name. The self is literally reborn in your children. Your pattern is incorporated into their being. So don't allow your "self" and your identity to be lost to outside influences.

Model Religion

Anything that plays an active role in your life plays an active role in the lives of your children as well. Conversely, anything that plays a passive role in your life is likely to play a passive role in theirs. The role that religion will play in their lives depends largely on the role it plays in yours, the parents. Their overall perception, however, is also shaped by the role that religion plays in society as a whole, and in this there are many mixed messages.

Love and unity are taught in all religions, yet, holier-than-thou separatism is practiced instead. No two denominations can agree on doctrine, much less any two religions. Heinous atrocities are committed in the name of God on a global scale, even as you read this sentence. No one has ever seen heaven or hell, God or a devil, and the price paid for a spiritual life is hard to justify when measured in worldly dollars and "sense".

Religion does not sell itself. People sell religion, and you must sell it to your children through example. It must be real, it must have substance and relevance. It must be congruent and clear. It must offer peace and solutions. It must tell them who they are, why they're here, and where they're going. Scripture must be a personal message addressed to the reader directly from his Creator, free of editing or human ego. Doctrine must be consistent with the Oneness of God and blessings must be evident.

> *"Are they waiting to see if the angels come to them, or thy Lord? The day that certain of the Signs of thy Lord do come, no good will it do to a soul to believe in them then, if it believed not before nor earned righteousness through its faith. Say: 'Wait ye: we too are waiting.' As for those who divide their religion and break up into sects, thou hast no part in them in the least: their affair is with Allah: He will in the end tell them the truth of all that they did. He that doeth good shall have ten times as much to his credit: He that doeth evil shall only be recompensed according to his evil: No wrong shall be done unto (any of) them."*
> *(Q 6:158-160)*

> *"...And if anyone earns any good, We shall give him an increase of good in respect thereof: for Allah [God] is oft-forgiving, most ready to appreciate (service)...And He listens to those who believe and do deeds of righteousness, and gives them increase of His Bounty...If Allah were to enlarge the provision for His servants, they would indeed transgress beyond bounds through the earth; but He sends (it) down in due measure as He pleases. For He is with His servants well-acquainted, watchful."*
> *(Q 42:23-27).*

PRACTICAL MATTERS

Flesh

The "you" that dwells within your body is constantly at war with the flesh. The flesh should submit to the soul, but often times it would rather submit to any worldly sensation that it finds pleasing at the moment. Imagine the flesh totally out of control, unrestrained. Most would agree that such a thing would be disastrous! Pedophiles would seize your children, alcohol and drugs would seize you both, unhealthy food would seize your heart, violent tendencies would seize your community, and people in power would seize your assets!

It's like a Jeckyll and Hyde syndrome where the higher self strives to keep the lower self contained within certain limits. The flesh always wants one more bite, one more minute, one more time, one more million, one more high, that man's wife ,and whatever else appeals to it. The flesh has no conscience. God has given the flesh the wisdom to know its own limits, but the wisdom of good and evil He put in your soul. And you gain strength through struggle, through the exercise of your conscience, like strengthening a muscle. If given the choice, most hearts would choose to submit to God, but the reality of the fleshly needs and desires are more tangible and more available than the spiritual counterparts. Submission demands selflessness. The lustful, evil mind wants to corrupt your soul by way of your flesh. Thousands of years have been devoted to refining the science of corrupting and exploiting the flesh. This world is obsessed with fleshly gratification in one form or another. It has mastered the art of seduction on every level.

> "...When they do aught that is shameful, they say: 'We found our fathers doing so'; and 'Allah commanded us thus;' Say: 'Nay, Allah [God] never commands what is shameful: do ye say of Allah what ye know not?'"
> (Q7:27-28).

GOD IS IN THE HEAVENS OF YOUR MIND

We must constantly keep ourselves in a mode of awareness and in the protecting guidance of God. This means sacrificing self-awareness to the degree that the body is in tune with the soul, and the soul is in tune with God-- "Reality Consciousness".

Part 4
THE PATH

Spiritual Milk

People want to see God face to face. They want to hear His voice crackle in the clouds. They want to fathom the unfathomable! Consider the newborn. As a newborn, you cannot grasp the meaning of things. Eventually your brain develops the ability to process information and sensory perception. You pick up language skills. God has made you in such a way that you develop in stages.

Spiritually, the same is true. You spend your appointed time in the spiritual womb before your spiritual birth takes place. You're born eyes closed knowing no more than your immediate needs. Eventually, your spiritual intelligence learns to process the stuff being picked up through your spiritual senses. You become aware of yourself and your environment and your connection to your Creator. Then you pick up language skills by listening to the "voice" of your Creator. Among other things, that voice is Qur'an.

A small child can speak the language of his parents, but it takes many years before he can really grasp the depths and subtleties of that language. Even more so with the Qur'an, because it deals with the unfathomable— God! Nevertheless, in it, He introduces Himself, reveals the meaning of things, the meaning of life, the meaning of you, gives you a history lesson and tells you about the future. In it, He gives guidance for good in this life and life in the Hereafter. It is a public registry of "Who's Who". It is a constitution of law and rights with perfectly balanced scales. It is a "will" establishing your divine inheritance. It is illumination in the darkness and confusion of worldly and spiritual affairs. It is a map for every lost soul.

The Qur'an is not the only word of God to be recorded by man, but it is the confirmation and completion of all prior revelations. It is clear in its basic message. Your soul wants what is in the Qur'an, but the Satanic mind wants what's in your soul— submission!

> "O ye who believe! Intoxicants and gambling, (dedication of) stones, and (divination by) arrows, are an abomination of Satan's handiwork: Eschew such (abomination), that ye may prosper: Satan's plan is (but) to excite enmity and hatred between you, with intoxicants and gambling, **and hinder you from remembrance of Allah, and from prayer:** will ye not then abstain?"
> (Q 5:90-91)

> "And Satan will say when the matter is decided: 'It was Allah Who gave you a promise of truth: I too promised, but I failed in my promise to you. I had no authority over you except to call you, but ye listened to me: then reproach not me, but reproach your own souls. I cannot listen to your cries, nor can ye listen to mine' "
> (Q 14:22).

Who Are You?

A human being comes into existence. Who can tell him who he is and how he came to be and why he is here- another human being who himself received second-hand information? Who has the knowledge of the "beginning"? Only someone who was present **before** the beginning can testify about the beginning! Who can tell you who you are besides the one who created you?

The Satanic mind wants to cut you off from that knowledge, thereby cutting you off from your strength. Remember, knowledge is potential, knowledge is power. A lifetime spent in the pursuit of knowledge is a small price to pay for an eternity of blessings made possible by that knowledge.

Knowledge, Then What?

Every soul is accountable for what it knows. Heavenly knowledge must be made a way of life. Many people talk the holy talk, but walk a crooked walk! We're only human and inevitably we err, but we live in a so-called Judeo-Christian society where fornication is the norm! And so are drinking, and government-owned and operated casinos (lottery and such), and lying, and televised gossip, and coveting, and endless abuses of all kinds, just to name a few.

We must bring our knowledge, or Reality Consciousness, to a level of action. We must enter into a sacred covenant with God. But you cannot make a covenant with God without understanding His terms. The one who fornicates, drinks, gambles, lies, gossips, covets, abuses, or feeds into any type of idolatry, cannot identify himself or herself with God. How lightly we take these matters. The law is clear in matters some of us transgress regularly! It's difficult to distinguish the House of God from the house of Satan sometimes. Many are disillusioned with religion and its inability to deliver on its promises, but how can it deliver when it's not true religion we practice?

So first comes Reality Consciousness, then the covenant, then the total way of life. If you honor your promise to God, He will honor His promise to you.

The Veil

It is not permissible to accept a part of the revelation and reject another.

> "*As to those who reject faith it is the same to them whether thou warn them or do not war them; they will not believe. Allah [God] hath set a seal on their hearts and on their*

hearing and on their eyes is a veil; great is the penalty they incur."
  (Q 2:5-6)

"To those who reject Our Signs and treat them with arrogance, no opening will there be of the gates of heaven, nor will they enter the Garden, until the camel can pass through the eye of a needle. Such is Our reward for those in sin."
  (Q 7:40)

People of this world identify with the material, and not much beyond that. They are blinded by the things they pursue. God has sealed their hearts with their own lusts and piled their material things so high as to veil their sight... **"nothing to man except that which he strives for".**

The one who is heedless of part of the book is like the one who is heedless of all of the book (the Qur'an or any divine scripture prior to Qur'an).

Religion is meant to be simple. God wants man to know Him. If we are pleasing to our Lord, our Lord will be pleasing to us. Foremost in pleasing our Lord is to recognize His exclusive right to be worshipped. No other can share this privilege. Neither sun nor moon, neither man nor angel can share God's glory.

The African American

Whatever ills befallen to society are magnified in the African-American community. Split families, lagging behind in higher learning and discrimination at every turn are just some of the major deficits in this ethnic economy.

Spiritually, we have a European identity. That is, like America, we have inherited the European mind. Without critical examination of our current trends and belief system, we'll remain lost in the syndrome of identifying with wrong instead of right.

Signs For Those Who Consider

As we said, worldly knowledge is a steppingstone to heavenly knowledge. The world is like a vast treasure chest of wisdom, with precious diamonds and pearls just waiting to be picked from the earth and sea. Consider the mind-boggling variety of creatures God put here and the complexities of their behavior. On a scientific level, man has gained incalculable knowledge and benefit by understanding his environment. But merely understanding his environment would be of no avail if God had not made the environment subject to man. It is not by the might or wisdom of man that the world yields to his will, but by the might and wisdom of God.

As far as we know, no other creature on earth is sentient in the sense that we are, but every species possesses an intelligence all its own. We have a superiority complex. In our arrogance, we fail to realize that we owe everything to our environment and all the creatures in it. We pick knowledge out of the ground just like we pick fruits and vegetables. We gather wisdom from the sea like fishermen. Yet, we humans treat our precious earth like some kind of whore— for a meager investment, we have our way with her. And love is not even part of the equation.

> *"Do ye not see that Allah [God] has subjected to your (use) all things in the heavens and on earth and has made His bounties flow to you in exceeding measure (both) seen and unseen? Yet there are among men those who dispute*

> *about Allah without knowledge and without guidance and without a Book to enlighten them!"*
> *(Q 31:20)*

> *"Behold! In the creation of the heavens and the earth; in the alternation of the Night and the Day; in the sailing of the ships through the Ocean for the profit of mankind; in the rain which Allah sends down from the skies, and the life which He gives therewith to an earth that is dead; in the beasts of all kinds that He scatters through the earth; in the change of the winds, and the clouds which they trail like their slaves between the sky and the earth- (here) indeed are Signs for a people that are wise."*
> *(Q 2:164)*

If we can gain such incalculable benefit by cooperating with our environment, imagine what progress could be made if we cooperate with each other. Everyone has some valuable contribution to make. Every human being is a potential asset. Consider how integrated all of nature is and how well-balanced it is maintained without the help of man. The earth is a prosperous, bountiful living organism of which we are an integral part. In it, is wisdom and resources for our social and physical well-being. When you achieve Reality Consciousness, or God-awareness, your relationship with your whole environment changes. In nature are signs for a people who are wise.

Woman

This is a difficult issue to deal with considering the inequities women have always endured in our male-dominated world, but again, God has established everything in due proportion. All we need to do is obey. God has left nothing haphazard or self-determining.

THE PATH

To reiterate a point made earlier, society for the most part, is lost in a syndrome[2] where right is wrong and wrong is right.

For example, a child who is raised among hate-mongers bent on racial genocide, like Nazi Germany, does not know that killing someone because they happen to be Jewish is wrong. This may seem like an extreme example, but understanding the principle behind it is critical if we are sincere about submitting to God's will. If history has taught us anything at all, it taught us that a group of people can be led to believe and agree on anything, and can be made to do anything, no matter how wrong, absurd, obscene, or vile. From this alone, we come closer to trusting in God. If left to man, confusion, chaos, disunity, injustice, and inequity ensue. If left to man, the relationship between man and woman is determined by social trends, and friction arises between the struggle of egos.

Man cannot effectively govern his affairs without guidance from the One who created him. The one qualified to instruct the user, is the inventor. *"It is He Who created you from a single person, and made his mate of like nature, in order that he might dwell with her (in love)" (Q 7:189).* So, who is best to determine the fate of man or woman other than the One who put them together in the first place?

Every man and every nation has an obligation to God to treat women justly, with kindness and respect. It's no accident that this is a male-dominated world, but tremendous responsibility comes with that territory.

> *"Men are protectors and maintainers of women, because Allah [God] has given the one more (strength) than the other, and because they support them from their means..."*
> *(Q 4:34)*

---

2. a distinctive characteristic or pattern of behavior; a group of symptoms that collectively indicate or characterize a disease, a psychological disorder, or another abnormal condition distinctive characteristic or pattern of behavior; a group of symptoms that collectively indicate or characterize a disease, a psychological disorder, or another abnormal condition.

GOD IS IN THE HEAVENS OF YOUR MIND

This does not give man license of superiority, but at his best, he is endowed with qualities better suited for the role of leadership, to assume the responsibility for the direction, character, and well-being of his family. A man's ranking with God is no higher than the treatment he shows his wife. A society ranks no higher than the stature of its women. Women are highly regarded in scripture, and are to be given their due.

In God's order of things, women are subordinate to men, but not inferior. Neither are they servants to men. But consider the relationship. Man's physical capacity exceeds the woman's. Why? Not so he can dominate her, but rather to spare her from the greater burdens in life. Psychologically as well, man has a higher threshold for bearing burdens, a necessary quality for various rigors of life. He can't do it alone obviously, but man's character and nature drive him to build and govern. Male and female share the same qualities to different degrees appropriate for their respective roles. A woman's first duty is to submit to God, and her second duty is to submit to the mate to whom God entrusted her well-being. The word "husband" really means "caretaker". It's more than a privilege, it's a trust from God. Any man who wrongs his woman, wrongs his own soul...

> "...nor should ye treat them with harshness...live with them on a footing of kindness and equity..."
> *(Q 4:19)*

Many women, understandably, have trouble with the idea of submitting to men. Many feel it is a tool of the arrogant and paternal chauvinism that pervades the male psyche. In other words, all this stuff has gone to his head. Women have always been treated like second-class human beings, as if they are lower than men. The notion that a woman's place is in the home was concocted in the minds of men. God never instructed men to keep their women at home or out of the workplace.

Men of sincere devotion to God and heart of understanding revere the intention behind God's design in placing man at the head of the table and placing the womb inside of the woman instead of the man. A woman rebels against God if she rebels against this divine arrangement.

How is it women follow political leadership, or corporate leadership, or cult leadership, but reject husband leadership? Why is it that women give more credence to the fluctuations of public sentiment than the eternal and supreme sentiment and wisdom of God? When two captains command the same ship, they rip the ship in half in their struggle with the steering wheel.

> *"Every kingdom divided against itself is brought to desolation..."*
> *(Luke 11:17)*

The union should be between souls of like nature. In this way, a woman would be comfortable, even pleased with her husband's leadership. She must choose someone with whom she is in sync, worthy of her loyalty. She, in turn, must be worthy of his emotional, spiritual and physical investment in her.

The Virtues of Islam

Muhammad came to a place and time of a backward people given to iniquity: tribal pride and warfare, polytheism, unimaginable sexual perversions and abuses, baby girls buried alive for no other reason than that they were female. These were people perched upon formidable hills of their own immoral filth, driven by greed, lust, violence, and ignorance.

GOD IS IN THE HEAVENS OF YOUR MIND

Muhammad was forty years old when his divine mission began, and by the time he died at the age of sixty-three, a new society had been born. And so began a new era for all mankind. Even if you don't embrace the teachings of Islam, you must concede its virtues. Unless your belief system and your moral make up are so contrary, you must admit that the world is elevated another notch for every person who embraces Islam and applies it in their lives. And there are approximately one billion Muslims across the globe, elevating the world by one billion notches! If one man (Muhammad) can elevate and enlighten one-fifth of the world population and turn them into God-fearing people, imagine what one billion can do with God behind them.

However, before joining the "revolution", one must successfully navigate the revolution in his or her own life. As the saying goes, get your own house in order first— self, family, home, your earnings, your community, and so on.

The Call

Let us strive to be a collective of finely-tuned individuals patterned after the best of us, the prophets. The first step is to step outside of the false reality that surrounds us, and into Reality Consciousness that comes from being God-centered.

God is literally in the heavens of your being. This is difficult to grasp, even for the most enlightened of us, but by tuning yourself to the One Reality the veils become more transparent.

Man wants to meet God face to face. We cannot gaze upon God directly, but we can gaze upon His image...
just look within yourself!